empower

publishing

Dianne Nicholas Goodrich

Illustrations by
Anna McCullough

empower

publishing

Empower Books
PO Box 26701
Winston-Salem, NC 27114

This book is a work of non-fiction. Names, characters, locations, events, and images are faithfully reproduced as reported and rendered by the author and not a result of the publisher or publishing process.

First Empower Books edition published
November 2020

Empower Books, Feather Pen, and all production design are trademarks of Indigo Sea Press, used under license.

Dianne Nicholas Goodrich, Author
Anna McCullough, Illustrator, a senior at Davie County High School. She plans to attend Liberty University and major in Graphic Art.

Edited and Interior Layout Design by Dr. Linda Fox Felker, President, Felker Consulting, Inc., Winston-Salem, NC 27103

Manufactured in the United States America
ISBN 978-1-63066-510-4

Dedicated to George and Joyce,

good friends for over 30 years.

Starr's Scary Adventure

My name is Starr. This name was given to me when I was born. My mother saw a white spot on my hip that looked like a star.

Mother and I live in the woods near a large farm. There is a white house and lots of noisy animals in a field nearby with tall grass.

One day, Mom and I heard Farmer George talking to his wife, Joyce. He said that he planned to cut their grass in a few days.

We did not really understand all that they were saying, but soon we would find out!

My mother went to the field to feed on blackberries, green briars, and saplings. I was too young to go with her, so I stayed behind to take a nap. My mother made me a nest to keep me snuggly warm.

When I was four weeks old, my mother said, “Starr, it is time for you to go with me to search for food.”

This was exciting news! I could hardly wait to go on this new adventure with my mother.

When we arrived at the field, my mother told me to lie down in the grass and wait. She was going to make sure there were no predators nearby.

I obeyed her and quietly nestled into the warm grass. A cozy feeling wrapped around me as I lay there.

As I fell asleep, George hopped up on the bush hog tractor mower to cut grass in the field.

As George started to mow, he saw a large deer stand up and run off into the woods. This startled him, but he continued to mow. He did not know that I was in the midst of the grass.

George circled around with the mower, and as he did, he looked down and saw a beautiful brown baby deer.

My terrified eyes looked up at him, but I did not move an inch.

I was frightened by the loud sounds and I was frozen in place.

Someone was protecting me because, if George had not seen me when he did, he would have run over me with the mower.

I thought about how my first visit to the field was supposed to be an exciting adventure, but it had turned into a scary one.

When George saw me, he quickly moved the tractor in a different direction. My mother saw the whole thing happen. She looked for an opportunity to rescue me.

After George left, my mother came to the field and took me back to the peaceful woods.

This was my Home Sweet Home, and I was so happy and thankful.

Holy
Bible

George parked the mower next to his house and rushed inside to tell Joyce the story about how a baby deer was saved from a sure death.

As he finished talking to his wife, a few Bible verses came to his mind. The verses from Job 12:7-12 tells us that “in the hand of the Lord is the life of every living thing.”

George knew that God’s hand was on me, that baby deer. God’s protection covered me, as it does all His creations.

Be thankful for God’s hand of protection. He provides for us every day of our lives.

About the Author

Dianne Nicholas Goodrich was born in Hampton, Virginia. She taught and worked with young children for over 29 years.

She and her husband, Timothy W. Goodrich, have been married for 46 years. They have two grown children, a son Stephen, and a daughter, Mary Beth. They also have three grandchildren, Gracyn, Waylon, and Keeley.

Dianne and Tim still enjoy teaching students in a Christian school in Lexington, NC. They are members of Sheets Memorial Baptist Church.

www.ingramcontent.com/pod-product-compliance
Lightning Source LLC
LaVergne TN
LVHW070224110826
845147LV00003B/636

9781630665104